Smithsonian

THE NATIONAL MUSEUM OF
NATURAL
HISTORY

BY SALLY LEE

CAPSTONE PRESS
a capstone imprint

Smithsonian is published by Capstone Press,
1710 Roe Crest Drive, North Mankato, Minnesota 56003
www.mycapstone.com

Library of Congress Cataloging-in-Publication Data
Names: Lee, Sally, 1943– author.
Title: The National Museum of Natural History / by Sally Lee.
Description: North Mankato, Minnesota : Capstone Press, 2018. | Series: Smithsonian field trips
| Includes bibliographical references and index.
Identifiers: LCCN 2017011303| ISBN 9781515779780 (library binding) | ISBN 9781515779896 (pbk.)
| ISBN 9781515780076 (ebook pdf)
Subjects: LCSH: National Museum of Natural History (U.S.)—Juvenile literature. | Natural history
museums—Washington (D.C.)—Juvenile literature.
Classification: LCC QH70.U62 W275 2018 | DDC 508.753—dc23
LC record available at https://lccn.loc.gov/2017011303

Editorial Credits
Michelle Hasselius, editor; Sarah Bennett, designer; Kelli Lageson, media researcher;
Laura Manthe, production specialist

Our very special thanks to Kealy Gordon, Product Development Manager; and Ellen Nanney, Licensing Manager,
Smithsonian, for their assistance. Capstone would also like to thank the following at Smithsonian Enterprises:
Brigid Ferraro, Vice President, Education and Consumer Products; Carol LeBlanc, Senior Vice President, Education,
and Consumer Products; and Christopher A. Liedel, President.

Photo Credits
©2017 National Museum of Natural History, Smithsonian: cover (top images), 3, 5, 7, 8 (top and bottom right), 9
(top left and top right), 10 (all), 11 (top), 14, 15 (bottom), 16 (bottom left), 17 (top right and bottom), 18 (all), 19,
20 (bottom), 21 (bottom left and bottom right), 22 (right), 23 (middle left, middle right, and bottom), 24 (right), 25
(top), 26 (left), 29 (left); Capstone Press: 15 (top); Courtesy NASA/JPL-Caltech, 20 (top); Getty Images: Allentown
Morning Call/Harry Fisher, 25 (bottom), Bettmann, 27, Michael Loccisano, 12; Newscom: ZUMA Press/NOAA, 11
(bottom); Shutterstock: 3d brained, 9 (bottom), ALong, 29 (right), Christophe BOISSON, 27 (design element),
Galyna Andrushko, 28 (bottom), gary yim, 21 (top), Herschel Hoffmeyer, 16 (middle), ingehogenbijl, 23 (design
element), iravgustin, 24 (bottom left), Kamira, cover (bottom), 6, Marco Rubino, 4 (bottom), Michael Rosskothen,
13, Oewsiri, 8 (bottom left), redboxart, 26 (right), Rich Carey, 17 (background), Tinnaporn Sathapornnanont, 4
(top), Vadim Sadovski, 20 (middle), Wlad74, cover (design element, used throughout); Thinkstock: AmandaLewis,
22 (bottom left); Wikimedia: Harriman Alaska series, 28 (top)

Printed in the United States of America.
010399F17

Table of Contents

Nature's Museum

The National Museum of Natural History is in Washington, D.C. With more than 145 million items, the Museum has the largest natural history collection in the world. Only some of the items are on display. The Museum's collection is used for research and to teach the public about the natural world.

—Fact—

The National Museum of Natural History holds more than 90 percent of all the Smithsonian's collections.

⬆ the tropical aquarium at the National Museum of Natural History

Did You Know?

The Museum is part of the Smithsonian Institution, which has 19 museums, nine research centers, and the National Zoo.

W lcoming l phant

An African elephant has greeted guests to the Museum since 1959. A Hungarian big-game hunter named Josef J. Fénykövi donated the elephant's skin to the Smithsonian. It weighed more than 2 tons (1.8 metric tons).

Taxidermists spent 16 months preparing the elephant for display. They made a life-size model out of 10,000 pounds (4,536 kilograms) of clay. They worked in a plastic house filled with steam to keep the clay from drying out. The model is 14 feet (4.3 meters) high and weighs about 12 tons (10.9 metric tons).

⬇ In 1959 the elephant was the world's largest land mammal displayed in a museum.

Did You Know?

The elephant's tusks weighed 90 pounds (40.8 kg). They were too heavy for the model. They were replaced with lighter tusks made of fiberglass.

↑ The elephant, nicknamed Henry, is located in the *Kenneth E. Behring Family Rotunda.*

Giant Squid

Two giant squid are on display in the Museum's *Sant Ocean Hall*. One was caught in a fisherman's net off the coast of Spain. The other is from a Spanish museum.

Giant squid are about 35 feet (10.7 m) long, with eight arms and two long feeding tentacles. People rarely see giant squid alive because they live so deep in the ocean. The Museum gives visitors the chance to see these animals up close.

—Fact—
The squid are kept in liquid tanks to preserve them.

⬇ The average adult man is 1/5th the size of a giant squid.

➡ museum specialist Mike Sweeney (left), curator Clyde Roper (center), and forklift operator Charles Beggs examine a giant squid in February 1983

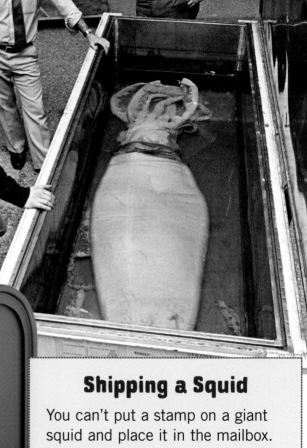

Did You Know?

Giant squid have the largest eyes in the animal kingdom. They help the squid see in the dark water.

Shipping a Squid

You can't put a stamp on a giant squid and place it in the mailbox. The squid at the Museum arrived in special airtight tanks full of water. They were wrapped in cloth and strapped in to keep their bodies and tentacles in place.

Phoenix the Whale

A 45-foot (14-m) model of Phoenix, a North Atlantic right whale, hangs in the *Sant Ocean Hall*. It was built in seven pieces and put together inside the Museum.

Phoenix was chosen as the Museum's model because scientists knew so much about her. They have followed Phoenix since she was born in 1987. Phoenix has had at least three calves. One of her calves, Smoke, gave birth in 2007.

← Scientists named the whale after a mythical bird from ancient Egypt.

Did You Know?

In 1997 Phoenix was tangled in a fishing net and almost died. The net left a scar below her right lip. Scientists added Phoenix's scar to the Museum's model.

—Fact—

Adult right whales like Phoenix weigh about as much as 12 African elephants.

Almost Extinct

The North Atlantic right whale is one of the most endangered whales in the world. Early seamen called these whales the "right" whales to hunt. They are large, slow, and usually stay near the shore. So many right whales have been killed that they almost became extinct. Today U.S. laws are in place to protect the whales, but their population remains small.

11

Titanoboa the Monster Snake

Sixty million years ago, northern Colombia was a jungle. It was home to Titanoboa, the largest snake that ever lived. The snake was more than 40 feet (12 m) long. It was longer than a city bus!

smithchan.com/monstersnake
#mo_stersnake

Titanoboa was discovered in 2007. The snake's backbones were found in a coal mine in Colombia. At first scientists thought the bones came from a crocodile. They couldn't believe such large bones belonged to a snake. Snakes grow larger in warmer climates. Scientists now believe extremely hot temperatures helped Titanoboa grow so large.

↑ The Titanoboa exhibit is no longer at the Smithsonian. It was a temporary exhibit that is currently traveling to other museums in the country.

—Fact—

Titanoboa weighed about 1.25 tons (1.13 metric tons).

Hatcher the Digital Triceratops

The very first Triceratops model went on display at the Museum in 1905. The bones were discovered in Wyoming in the late 1880s. More than 90 years later, the Triceratops needed a makeover. A visitor looking at the dinosaur let out a loud sneeze. The model was so fragile that the sneeze caused a piece of bone to break and fall to the floor! To fix the model, researchers scanned each of the dinosaur's 200 bones using a 3-D scanner. Scientists then printed copies of the bones on a 3-D printer.

Did You Know?

In 2001 the restored model was named "Hatcher" after John Bell Hatcher, a paleontologist who discovered the fossils.

TRICERATOPS

Time:	66–68 million years ago
Ate:	Plants
Length:	Up to 30 feet (9 m)
Weight:	13,000 to 22,000 pounds (6 to 9 metric tons)

—Fact—

Hatcher is the world's first dinosaur to have all its bones recorded and created in 3-D.

Modern Fossils

Studying fossils is easier today thanks to 3-D scanners. The scanners use beams of laser light and two cameras to record the size and shape of each fossil. The data can be shared with others or used to print 3-D copies of the fossils in any size. By using small 3-D copies, experts can study how dinosaurs moved without harming the real bones.

⬇ Triceratops skull

Whale Graveyard

In 2010 highway workers in Chile uncovered a whale graveyard. It held the fossils of at least 40 prehistoric whales. The bones were stacked in layers. This meant the whales died the same way in the same place over several thousand years.

Scientists wondered what killed them. But since the bones were found in the middle of a construction project, scientists only had a few weeks to search for clues. They had to scan many of the bones in the ground. Scientists found bits of orange algae on some of the fossils. They concluded that the algae were toxic and had poisoned the whales. Toxic algae still kills many marine animals today.

↑ one of the whale fossils discovered in Chile

The Smithsonian made a 3-D print of one of the whale skeletons. *"It's the largest 3D print of its kind in the world."*
—Smithsonian scientist Nick Pyenson

⬆ a fossil of a rorqual whale found in Cerro Ballena, Chile

The Hope Diamond

The Hope Diamond is one of the Museum's most popular attractions. In 1668 King Louis XIV of France bought a 115-carat diamond from a merchant named Jean Baptiste Tavernier. The stone was called "Blue Diamond of the Crown" and "French Blue." The king wore the stone on a neck ribbon during ceremonies. After the French Revolution, the French government kept the stone until it was stolen in September 1792.

The Hope Diamond turned up again in England in 1812. But it had been cut down to 45.52 carats. Over the next hundred years, several wealthy people owned the diamond. Jeweler Harry Winston bought the diamond in 1911. He donated it to the Smithsonian in 1958.

The Curse

Some believe the Hope Diamond is cursed. King Louis XVI had the diamond in 1765, when he became king of France. He was beheaded along with Queen Marie Antoinette in 1793. Other owners of the diamond have been murdered, had terrible accidents, or lost their fortunes. Some people believe that even the postal carrier who delivered the stone to the Smithsonian was cursed. Soon after James Todd delivered the Hope Diamond to the Museum, his leg was crushed in a truck accident. He also injured his head in a car accident, and his house burned to the ground.

⬆ The Hope Diamond is displayed on a rotating pedestal in the *Harry Winston gallery.*

➡ Winston sent the Hope Diamond to the Museum by registered first-class mail. The package that the gem arrived in is now part of the Smithsonian's collection.

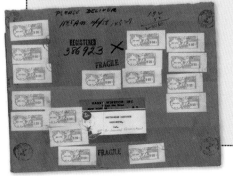

—Fact—

The Hope Diamond is named after Henry Phillip Hope. His family owned the diamond from 1830 to 1901.

Meteorites from Mars

Meteorites are pieces of rock or metal from space. They fall to Earth without burning up in the Earth's atmosphere. They come from larger objects in our solar system, such as planets. Some of the meteorites in the Museum come from Mars. Scientists know this because the rocks contain the same gases found on Mars.

↑ Mars

⬇ This is known as the "life on Mars" meteorite. Discovered in Antarctica, it is 4.1 billion years old. It is the oldest meteorite from Mars at the Museum.

—Fact—

Most meteorites come from an area between the orbits of Mars and Jupiter.

Antarctica is the best place to find meteorites. Its cold, dry climate preserves them. Scientists visit Antarctica every year to collect meteorites.

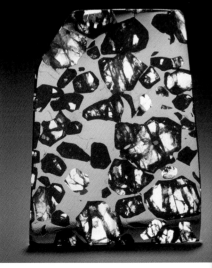

↑ This pallasite meteorite was found in Argentina. It's made of iron-nickel metal and a green material called olivine.

← a meteorite found in Texas

Egyptian Mummy

There are several Egyptian artifacts at the Museum. Ancient Egyptians believed that they would live on in another world after they died. If they were pharaohs or other wealthy people, their bodies were preserved as mummies for that world.

To make a mummy, a priest would remove the organs from the body. Even the brains were removed — through the nose! Then the body was covered with a natural salt to dry out. Afterward the dried body was wrapped in strips of linen. Finally the mummy was placed in a stone coffin called a sarcophagus.

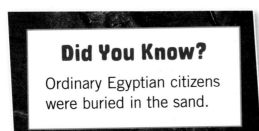

Did You Know?

Ordinary Egyptian citizens were buried in the sand.

➡ the mummy of an Egyptian man who died 2,000 years ago

Mummy X-Rays

Modern tools have changed the way mummies are studied today. X-rays and CT scans let scientists study fragile mummies without unwrapping them. These tools help experts learn about ancient diseases and treatments. Scientists can also study bones to help them determine the mummy's age or height. Scientists can often tell how the mummy died as well.

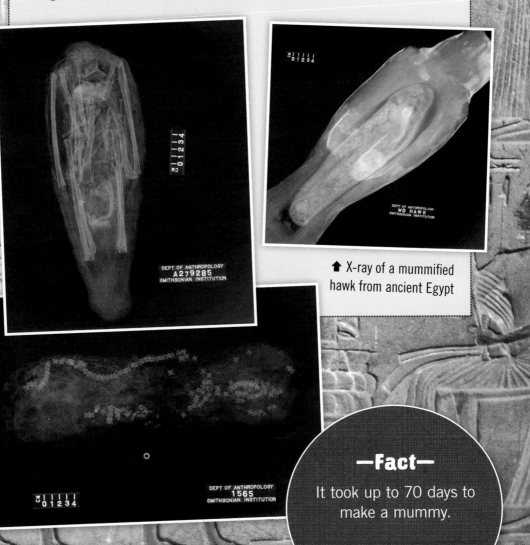

DEPT OF ANTHROPOLOGY
A279285
SMITHSONIAN INSTITUTION

DEPT OF ANTHROPOLOGY
WD HAWK
SMITHSONIAN INSTITUTION

⬆ X-ray of a mummified hawk from ancient Egypt

DEPT OF ANTHROPOLOGY
1565
SMITHSONIAN INSTITUTION

—Fact—

It took up to 70 days to make a mummy.

Soap Man

In 1875 construction workers found a coffin in Philadelphia, Pennsylvania. When the coffin was opened, the man's body inside had turned to soap! Over time, water had leaked into the coffin, carrying salts from the ground. The water and salt mixed with the fat in the man's body and turned it into soap.

➡ Soap Man was well-preserved. You can still see the knee-high stockings he was buried in!

—Fact—
Soap is made with water, fat, and salt.

↑ In addition to Soap Man, fragile mummies and coffins are stored in the Museum's *Dry Environment room*.

Did You Know?

Another body found near Soap Man had also turned to soap. Soap Lady is located at the Mutter Museum in Philadelphia.

Soap Man is too fragile to be on display. He is stored in a special glass case in the Museum's *Dry Environment room*. The temperature and moisture are controlled. Researchers study Soap Man to learn how chemical changes can preserve the human body.

World's Longest Beard

Hans Langseth entered a beard contest when he was 19 years old. When the contest was over, he continued to grow his beard. Langseth's beard was listed in the *Guinness Book of World Records* as the longest beard in the world. When he died in 1927 at age 81, Langseth's beard was 17 feet 6 inches (5 m 15.2 centimeters) long. After his death his family donated the beard to the Smithsonian, where it is kept in storage.

Did You Know?

Beard hair can only grow 4 or 5 feet (1 or 1.5 m) before it dies. Langseth kept the hair in his beard coiled together. That way it wouldn't fall out.

⬆ physical anthropologists Lucille St. Hoyme (left), J. Lawrence Angel (center), and Thomas Dale Stewart (right) hold Langseth's beard after it is delivered to the Smithsonian in 1967

—Fact—

Langseth showed off his beard in a traveling circus for a short time.

From Scientist to Specimen

Robert Kennicott was a naturalist at the Smithsonian from 1852 to 1866. Later he became one of its specimens.

In 1866 Kennicott was found dead while on an expedition to Alaska. People thought he killed himself with a poison called strychnine, but it was never proven. More than 130 years later, Smithsonian scientists used modern technology to find out how the naturalist died. They studied Kennicott's skeleton and medical history. Their tests showed that Kennicott didn't kill himself. He most likely died of a heart condition. Kennicott was so important to the Smithsonian that his family let the Museum keep his body in their collection.

⬇ Explorer-scientists Robert Kennicott (back left), Henry Ulke (back right), Henry Bryant (front right), and William Stimpson (front left) lived and worked at the Smithsonian in the 1850s and 1860s.

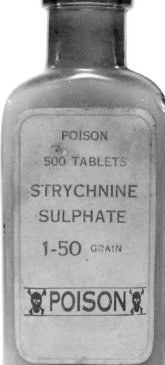

POISON
500 TABLETS
STRYCHNINE SULPHATE
1-50 GRAIN
☠POISON☠

—Fact—

During Kennicott's time, strychnine was taken in small amounts as medicine. Now we know it is poisonous.

29

Glossary

3-D (THREE-dee)—having length, width, and depth

algae (AL-jee)—small organisms that live in wet places and get their energy from the sun

carat (KAR-uht)—a unit for measuring the weight of precious gems and metals

extinct (ik-STINGKT)—no longer living; an extinct animal is one that has died out, with no more of its kind

fiberglass (FY-buhr-glas)—a strong, lightweight material made from thin threads of glass

laser (LAY-zur)—equipment that creates special beams of light

linen (LIN-uhn)—a cloth made from the flax plant

model (MOD-uhl)—something that is made to look like a person, an animal, or an object

naturalist (NACH-ur-uhl-ist)—someone who studies animals and plants

specimen (SPESS-uh-muhn)—a sample or example used to stand for an entire group

taxidermist (TAKS-uh-der-mist)—someone who prepares, stuffs, and mounts animal skins

tentacle (TEN-tuh-kuhl)—a long, armlike body part some animals use to touch, grab, or smell

tusk (TUHSK)—one of the pair of long, curved, pointed teeth of an elephant, a walrus, a wild boar, and other animals

Read More

Griffey, Harriet. *Secrets of the Mummies.* DK Readers. New York: DK Publishing, 2013.

Holtz, Jr., Thomas R. *Digging for Triceratops: A Discovery Timeline.* Dinosaur Discovery Timelines. North Mankato, Minn.: 2015.

Korrell, Emily B. *Awesome Adventures at the Smithsonian: The Official Kids Guide to the Smithsonian Institution.* Washington, D.C.: Smithsonian Books, 2013.

Critical Thinking Questions

1. Scientists use modern tools such as X-rays and CT scans to study a mummy without unwrapping it. What can scientists learn about a mummy from these tools?

2. In your own words, explain how a man's body turned to soap in Philadelphia.

3. After conducting modern tests, how do scientists believe naturalist Robert Kennicott died in 1866?

Internet Sites

Use FactHound to find Internet sites related to this book.

Visit *www.facthound.com*

Just type in 9781515779780 and go.

Check out projects, games and lots more at
www.capstonekids.com

Index